LATOYA LAWRENCE

God Has The Last Word

Beneficial Essentials: Reflective Devotional-Style Inspiration

Contents

One

My Input

I love to write. I have been writing since childhood.

I do not write just to be writing. I must be moved to write.

Whether it is by spirit, inclination, or both, the experience is beyond me.

From time to time there is an intermission, though, the ability and performance is always there.

But the essence of celestial flow has its frame of consistent exercise.

There was a rare time a while back where I did not think I would be interested in writing anymore.

I thought the thrill was gone but God showed me different.

For God is working in you, giving you the desire and the power to do what pleases him. –Philippians 2:13

When we are open to let the Lord work through us to fulfill our purpose, he will generate his power and continue to lead us down the correct path.

When we may believe we are finished or have no more to offer in a particular area due to mixed feelings, the Lord will unexpectedly surprise us by showing us that he is not yet done with us.

His silence or what seemed as a stagnation was just a reformation to an elevation.

* * *

He Did Not Forget

There is a lot to life that many of us know and a lot to life that many of us do not know since everything is not revealed to us on this side of the realm.

Some of us can peek into mysteries of the unknown through gifts of connection between the physical and spiritual dimensions, though God allows us to see and experience supernatural occurrences, we will never know the full picture until it is ultimately revealed by him.

Spiritual encounters build faith and implant wisdom through grasping firsthand learning along with keen intuitive perception.

As spirit writes through me one of my purposes is to fulfill my mission as a writer and messenger.

God gifts us with faculties, and he will inspire us to use them by instilling the drive, guidance, and direction when we follow his cues.

Now, we all have free will so God is not always responsible for our input or how me may handle or go about doing things, in general, but he is there steering the way and watching our backs when we acknowledge his authority and hand over our lives.

It is all about relationship when it comes to God. Not other people's opinion on how they judge what they falsely conceive or misunderstand about you- but what God knows about you in relation to him and where you both stand.

No one knows us better than God and he is the only one who can determine a person's heart and true intentions.

Do not worry about what others say or think about you, they have no power over you. People will judge you when they do not even know you.

It could be something you said without them knowing the full story or your full life story for why you may have spoken a certain way that they took out of context, and so on.

God knows the entire story and he is the one who writes the ending while opening new chapters.

Nobody's opinions, biases, misjudgments or whatever else reflects or diminishes God's presence within your life and your personal knowledge of him.

When certain people and certain life predicaments get on your last nerve, and you know deep down inside whatever appears to not be happening is meant to happen despite things looking the total opposite in not ever happening at all.

But you know as something within you yourself will not quit or give up in your way of thinking, believing- especially if you keep enhancing and there is nothing around you tangibly enhancing you to advance spiritually, mentally, physically or emotionally.

That is God's spirit inhabiting you, working through you to further enrich, upgrade, and magnify you.

And what he increases no one can decrease.

Others will get jealous or resentful at the fact God chooses certain people as vessels for whatever it is he intensely has designed for a special purpose.

They will take their unsettling attitudes out on you- but who cares!

People should be careful who they point fingers at because God may just have his anointed finger pointed at you.

The one who he will let rise for all to see how he demonstrated his glory directly through you.

God has not forgotten.

When you least expect what seemed like a condition that refused to ever budge- whatever it is concerning your matter or situation- he will suddenly come push that barrier out of the way because that block was a wall of protection until the coast was clear.

God was waiting until you were ready and prepared to emerge once he knocked down all obstacles to roll out his divine carpet for you to blessedly walk upon.

* * *

A Little Backstory Into My Forward Story To Us Who Apply

Reading and writing were my best subjects in school as a child.

I love to read and write.

I had the opportunity to get published through a mainstream publisher around the age of ten by a counselor of mine who showed my short stories I wrote back then to a colleague she knew who worked at a publishing company.

It was a compliment and an honor to get recognized at such a young age for my talent.

I knew when I was twelve, a writer I was, and a writer/book writer I wanted to be once I became an adult.

At the time I did not think my aspirations would ever come into fruition- not because I did not believe in myself- but because of circumstances going on around me at the time.

A lot of us know deep in our hearts while we are youngsters what our true callings in life are.

By the time I turned sixteen a lot had changed giving me a new outlook on life regarding my future and state of existence as a young girl coming up in the world where I had experienced unsavory family members who were extremely envious and jealous of the person I was and of the mother who raised me.

They were intent on holding us back to destroy our lives.

However, God had a different plan.

It was not an easy journey but one I made it through with the spirit of strength and an awesome mother who incredibly handled and survived all that she had to go through in her life by family members who tried to pull her down.

Mother and I stuck together with our beloved dog that we had since she was a puppy and all of us shared a love and a bond that no one could break.

We were also highly sensitive spiritual people, so our faith and awareness were always strong, discerning, and always rising above whatever negativity came our way through others who were incongruent or demonic.

As good people, a lot of other good people liked and loved us, and we had a lot of good times.

We loved to laugh.

We also enjoyed and treasured our passions and multi talents, something that kept us occupied along with other things as well.

No matter what situation came up in life or what we may have gone through from time to time nothing ever stopped us from being competent, capable, and confident in who we were and what we wanted to- or knew we could do.

So, regardless of life circumstances and events that take place that may seem grim where your dreams may seem impossible or sitting hot and boiling on the back burner of feeling held back- take heed.

Your pot is not overcooked, it was just warming up.

Two

Mission

A introduction of reflection by LaToya Lawrence- Originally Written December 2020

I rededicated my life to the Lord after being angry at him for approximately fifteen years and now that I have resumed a relationship with him I have been filled with the pleasant desire to use my platforms to share and help others through my Christian faith, and good news of the true gospel.

I am not a preacher or any spiritual leader I am just inspired and encouraged to write messages centered around our daily walk with God. *–And all of this is a gift from God, who brought us back to himself through Christ. And God has given us this task of reconciling people to him.*

For God was in Christ, reconciling the world to himself, no longer counting people's sins against them. And he gave us this wonderful message of reconciliation. So we are Christ's ambassadors; God is making his appeal through us. We speak for Christ when we plead, "Come back to God!" -2 Corinthians 5:18-20

For we speak as messengers approved by God to be entrusted with the Good News. Our purpose is to please God, not people. He alone examines the motives of our hearts. -Thessalonians 2:4

If we are afraid to offend people with the truth then God cannot use us to spread the gospel and to be an example of his testimony.

The gospel can indeed be offensive and there is no other way to approach or to get around this fact.

People would rather hear and listen to the lies from hell!

They would prefer to believe that it is okay to have grace from God and live within accordance to the devil. *–For a time is coming when people will no longer listen to sound and wholesome teaching. They will follow their own desires and will look for teachers who will tell them whatever their itching ears want to hear. -2 Timothy 4:3*

When is the last time we heard a blunt sermon from an evangelist who has access to reach across the nations through their fame and popularity? I cannot remember when there has been one bold enough to do so in years!

The preachers we see on television now are motivated by their high-pay and expensive lifestyles. They continue to water-down the gospel in order to maintain their fortune.

True believers are not inspired to seek out fame, money, or a title for themselves they are intent to preach about the consequences of sin, the importance of repentance and turning away from sin to live one's life for Jesus at the cost of forsaking one's self, and the world we live in.

There are even ministers in everyday churches that are not famous or well-known who are not preaching straightforward biblical truths. They have their own watered-down versions of what the gospel is too!

And now I make one more appeal, my dear brothers and sisters. Watch out for people who cause divisions and upset people's faith by teaching things contrary to what you have been taught. Stay away from them. Such people are not serving Christ our Lord; they are serving their own personal interests. By smooth talk and glowing words they deceive innocent people. -Romans 16: 17-18

No one will be genuinely saved through the words of a false gospel or one messaged with half-truths.

There are severe repercussions to endure and blood on the hands of those who deceitfully mislead and cause others to fall. God does not want false conversions due to those in authority not conveying what is really the true gospel. *–But if you cause one of these little ones who trusts in me to fall into sin, it would* *be better for you to have a large millstone tied around your neck and be drowned in the depths of the sea. -Matthew 18:6*

It is so important for people to take upon themselves by reading scripture to validate fact from fiction. Never listen to anyone or anything that is not backed up by the bible. Although everything possible does not have to be written in the Bible for it to be true!

Note: Some preachers or everyday people may understandably misinterpret scripture here and there and do not mean any harm within their utterances, however, there is always room for re-evaluation and correction.

In your journey, do not fear to stand up for truth and to not be persuaded by worldly comfort and worldly things to dilute the truth of God's word.

"Not everyone who calls out to me, 'Lord! Lord!' will enter the Kingdom of Heaven. Only those who actually do the will of my Father in heaven will enter. On judgment day many will say to me, 'Lord! Lord! We prophesied in your name and cast out demons in your name and performed many miracles in your name.' But I will reply, 'I never knew you. Get away from me, you who break God's laws.' -Matthew 7:21-23

* * *

It Does Not Have To Be Written In The Bible For It To Be True

From my observations throughout the years there are so-called Christians and others alike who believe if something is not written or mentioned within the Bible then the instance is unlikely to be true or not possible- which I know for fact has never been the truth.

Something does not have to be in the Bible for it to be truthful or possible.

Everything not written in the Bible that can occur is also not always devil inspired or people inspired either.

There is credibility to many situations, circumstances, encounters that were experiences not directly included as taken place in the Bible.

Some people are stuck in their limited scope of reasoning, narrow-mindedness, ignorance, brainwashing, or influences brought on by society.

That is why it is so important to be strong-minded and confident within one's own.

Knowing while certain others may not share an experience or a belief in no way will make another's experience or belief less probable.

There is a great possibility for their undergoing to be a reality and able to exist.

I have always been headstrong. I do not have to go through

something to believe or to know it is able to be true for someone else.

Maybe because I have that insight, nevertheless, one should never let others sway their minds or raise doubt in what they hold to know or believe firmly.

Of course, we as people are liable to hold onto false or erroneous ways of being.

Anyone can misinterpret or be mistaken about things it is when they fail to accept their error once they have discovered or have been proven to be wrong in some way.

Three

Life

Life is strange.

There are a lot of nice things in and about life, yet there is still great mystery and eeriness to the existence of it.

When I was a child, I wondered just like I am sure others have, where God came from.

There is no end and no beginning with him- this itself is haunting.

How did God materialize?

The question is beyond our comprehension, an instance we are not able to fathom or assimilate knowingly.

Our minds in this human experience are always looking for answers to satisfy the spirit as the spirit is in connection to more than what we are conscious of regardless of how spiritually awake or In tune we may be.

Even with our eyes fully open we need to get totally back to nature to be fed the proper nutrients

Just as our body and mind need to be fed healthily so does our spirit.

With things that seem unfamiliar there is still familiarity to them.

We were not strangers to the earth before we were born. We were already linked through the force of life within the power of God's thoughts upon us.

The fact that we were acknowledged by him before he created us into existence adds energy to the essence.

Spirituality is important no matter what one believes in, however, there is only one God whose name is Jehovah/Yahweh.

The father, the son (Jesus), and the Holy Spirit are one- the trinity.

We cannot maintain or sustain life without the life-giving force who gives to us life.

We all need God, and we all need to continuously pray.

For many, prayer is a last resort rather than an initial response.

Usually, after all accustomed options have exhausted the only thing left to do by those who are desperate is to call on God, even if beforehand they never had or sought out a personal relationship with the Lord.

Some people just speak to God on occasion to fulfill a special need or desire then forget about him and go on with their lives.

As a habit, many adapt to the conditions that they become familiar with and when things become complicated, or need fixing, the first direction in where they run to is what they rely on as it is primarily routine to them.

Prayer is a speed dial that accesses us to God's phone extension immediately.

His line is never busy, and he can take multiple calls at a time with no delay, interruption, or time limit.

Most of all, there is no charge, the exchange is totally free.

We are to use and take advantage of this offer and special deal constantly throughout the day to deliver and discuss any message of information to God for any reason.

Do not forget to thank the Lord for this kind and beneficial gesture along with the other vital, necessary, and generous blessings that he undeservingly hands out to us through his love.

Genuine followers of Jesus Christ know to consult directly through him to the father as the number one priority above all others.

Prayer is our intimate source of communication with the Lord, the immediate action to be taken before, within, and after any circumstance or situation.

Prayer is the key and faith unlocks the door.

When we have faith, we put all our trust in God.

So, we do not do like the world or worldly people do, placing hope and trust in the things created instead of the creator who activates everything that he creates.

Know who is truly in control and that the Lord is the only one who can completely work conditions out suitably and effectively to his plan.

Prayer is welcomed and encouraged by God always, and for all things.

He existed before anything else, and he holds all creation together. Christ is also the head of the church, which is his body. He is the beginning, supreme over all who rise from the dead. So he is first in everything. Colossians 1:17-18

Never stop praying. - 1 Thessalonians 5:17

Devote yourselves to prayer with an alert mind and a thankful heart. -Colossians 4:2

Search for the LORD and for his strength; continually seek him. -1 Chronicles 16:11

Do not be anxious about anything, but in every situation, by prayer and petition, with thanksgiving, present your requests to God. And the peace of God, which transcends all understanding, will guard your hearts and your minds in Christ Jesus. -Philippians 4:6-7

* * *

Call On The Lord

God is always available. He is ready, willing and able to help at all times.

He waits to hear our voice, whether we are eager or hesitant.

He wants us to call out to him within anticipation and without doubt.

There is no situation or circumstance that God cannot handle or resolve.

He does extraordinary work behind the scenes preparing everything together for our benefit.

No matter how difficult or tragic life may appear God is right there sharing in each moment.

He remains close beside us and deep within us.

As children of God, we are his forever, and he will never leave us or let us go- that is an absolute promise a reassurance to count on!

Don't be afraid, for I am with you. Don't be discouraged, for I am your God. I will strengthen you and help you. I will hold you up with my victorious right hand. -Isaiah 43:10

For I hold you by your right hand— I, the LORD your God. And I say to you, 'Don't be afraid. I am here to help you. Isaiah 43:13

* * *

New Life

Therefore if any man be in Christ, he is a new creature: old things are passed away; behold, all things are become new. -2 Corinthians 5:17

Those of us fortunate enough to have awaken to another day of life today have entered into another new year.

There is nothing greater to celebrate upon newness than to become a genuinely new creation in Jesus Christ.

These years on earth will eventually come to an end. This life we live here in the world now is only temporary.

Do you know where your spirit/soul will go and be once you depart from this life?

Why not let it be eternally spent with our wonderful heavenly father.

Instead of looking forward to new better years to come here on the earth- a place that is definitely not going to last- anticipate a future of greater hope and assurance by reserving a place truly to call home.

Let this new year be a time to accept Jesus Christ into your life. Totally surrender everything to him and get to receive his promises of love, security, and true life.

All that you have to do is honestly believe in him, tell him you want him to become your lord and savior, repent for all your wrong doing, allow his holy spirit that will come to dwell within you to help you obey his beneficial instructions for you, pray to him constantly and read your bible/scripture daily so that you develop a deep personal relationship with God and you will be on your way!

Thank and praise the Lord for his grace, mercy and pure goodness.

Be overjoyed for having made the best and most crucial decision of your life because you will have an eternity to be forever grateful for.

Above all, spend quality time with God.

Include him within everything you say and do. Let him continuously be your guide and provider, he will always come through.

Get to know God intimately.

You do this by talking to him (through prayer) and reading your bible/scripture as often as possible.

God loves you extremely, and he only wants the ultimate best for you and you will obtain this care by pure faith. Put all your trust in God then wait on him.

* * *

Adult Baptism

I was anointed by a priest with oil/holy water when I was an infant, and the event was very significant.

It served as both a blessing for me and an act of faith along with a belief in God on my mother's part.

My mother received a baptism of her own desire, a demonstration of dedication at ten years of age.

Growing up, my mother as well as a few pastors imparted that it wasn't necessary for me to be baptized again once I reached adulthood.

Of course, water baptism is not at all what saves one as "baptism of the spirit" is vital, and key point.

Accepting Jesus then receiving his Holy Spirit is what actually makes us "born again".

Water baptism is our outward display of commitment as followers/children of God.

After all of these years spirit inspired me to get baptized a second time around. I made the choice as I had already been chosen then led.

The pastor at the nondenominational church I attended advised me to write my own testimony as encouragement to others who would be present.

On the day of the ceremony, which took place just before Sunday service, I recited the sincere statement I had wrote.

After I finished, I received a strong unexpected hand of applause from the crowd.

In my written testimony I spoke:

I come from a family that always believed in God. At four months my mom had me christened/blessed in a Catholic church.

At two and a half years of age I learned to read so soon after my mother taught me to pray every night and introduced me to the Bible.

My mother, family, and I discovered very early that I had special spiritual gifts of dreams, visions, discernment and other things which gave me a natural propensity to be drawn toward God.

I first asked the Lord into my life personally between the age of ten to twelve and have experienced many deep and significant personal accounts and experiences of his insight, protection, life development, guidance and continued providence.

This baptism will be my adult step in expressing my outward diligence and appreciation within the faith and belief in recognizing the eternal life-giving love and power of the Lord, God.

Another thing I hadn't expected was for the tub of water the Pastor and I stood in to be so comfortably warm. This made my experience all the better to endure.

I was asked by the pastor If I accepted Jesus Christ as my Lord and Savior. I answered in return, "Of Course I do".

The pastor smiled and the crowd of attendees chuckled at my words.

"LaToya, I baptize you in the name of the Father, the Son, and the Holy Spirit", uttered the pastor.

Then immediately I was immersed into the waist-deep body of water.

It was beautiful.

I went into the bathroom to dry off and change my clothes so I could sit in for the sermon.

While I listened to the sermon one of the clergies handed me my baptismal certificate.

When church service came to an end a lady I've never met before rose from a seat and among the others to speak to the pastor who had preached.

I was sitting close by when they both walked over toward my way. She addressed to me, "God is using you in a very powerful way".

"And you too", she also acknowledged to the pastor.

I'd recommend to those who have not yet done so already to accept Jesus into their life and go get baptized.

Even if like me who initially sought a personal relationship with God during childhood just do it! It is never too late.

Baptism is truly wonderful.

* * *

Infant Christening/Baptism: A Lovely Event
I will repeat it again as I discuss the baptism of babies- *My mother wasted no time!*

She got me baptized/christened when I was four months old.

My mother herself, as a young church attendant, made the urgent decision to get baptized at ten years of age.

Baptism does not save one, though, it is a wonderful expression of our faith and devotion.

There are people who believe that infant christening/baptism is an insignificant or irrelevant event because the child has no knowledge yet of what is taking place or the faculty to decide whether to accept Jesus Christ.

People have the right to think or believe what they want.

However, I strongly disagree with this mode of thought, and I do not care what anyone else has to say about the matter.

There are fully grown people who partake in adult baptism with all their faculties in place, developed to ponder, select, choose, and determine- and their act of holy anointment will make no difference if their heart, mind, and soul are not lined up to what it means to demonstrate the outward representation of faith and the commitment to follow God's path.

So, whether a baby is not able to make the conscious profession of a belief in the crucified savior who was buried then resurrected for everyone's benefit to have eternal life- their holy christening/baptism is no less significant at all.

It is for some, as I know for a fact, an act of belief on the parent's part, to have their child blessed by God so that he may also have his hand on that child to supernaturally guide and lead them on the correct road to him.

It is the parent's beautiful expression of offering and celebrating their child or children into the hands and family of God himself.

***

Providence: My Great Protector

I noticed since early childhood the favor over my mother and I, and the manner in which God took great care of my family.

The Lord watched over us solicitously, his eyes vigilant to never waver, his hands fixed firmly on every situation. Even when I did not think or believe he was looking out or holding our circumstances in place.

We mattered to God. And, we still do.

I have been so very fortunate by his mercy and grace, covered by what seemed like an extra hedge of protection from others and the principalities of this evil world, and beyond.

When I look back, I see all that I avoided and escaped because of the wisdom and discernment granted upon me from the Lord.

The comfort and peace I experienced in the midst of trials that made people of the world marvel at me in disappointment and wonder.

Enemies or adversaries that attempted to destroy me were defeated.

Even so-called believers who professed to be Christians The Lord had warned and protected me against, wholeheartedly coming to my rescue to head me out into safety.

God is definitely my refuge and strength, an essential help in times of trouble as well as in times of order.

* * *

He Ascended The Destiny Of The Past, Present And Future

That is why the Scriptures say, "When he ascended to the heights, he led a crowd of captives and gave gifts to his people."

Notice that it says "he ascended." This clearly means that Christ also descended to our lowly world.

And the same one who descended is the one who ascended higher than all the heavens, so that he might fill the entire universe with. -Ephesians 4: 8-10

Even though by faith the saints of the Old Testament were saved they were not allowed to go directly into heaven immediately after dying prior to Jesus's death and resurrection.

The reason is because Jesus had not yet made atonement for our sins to be cleansed through his crucifixion.

In the meantime, God furnished the saints of the Old Testament in a part of Sheol which was called "Abraham's Bosom"- a comfortable atmosphere of peace and rest. There they would wait until Jesus arrived.

Within a separate (opposite) part of Sheol was a place of suffering and torment. This place was called Hades- where the souls of the unbelievers without faith, and wicked resided upon their deaths.

When Jesus died on the cross, he descended in the earth where he preached to the saints of the Old Testament while they continued to wait in Abraham's Bosom.

As the Messiah they in faith one day expected, he described to them God's plan of salvation then set them all free within three days after Jesus himself ascended into heaven by directly escorting them.

That is why the Good News was preached to those who are now dead—so although they were destined to die like all people, they now live forever with God in the Spirit. 1 Peter 4:6

Christ suffered for our sins once for all time. He never sinned, but he died for sinners to bring you safely home to God. He suffered physical death, but he was raised to life in the Spirit.

So he went and preached to the spirits in prison— 1 Peter 3:18-19

* * *

The Final Destination

This boasting will do no good, but I must go on. I will reluctantly tell about visions and revelations from the Lord.

I was caught up to the third heaven fourteen years ago.

Whether I was in my body or out of my body, I don't know—only God knows.

Yes, only God knows whether I was in my body or outside my body.

But I do know that I was caught up to paradise and heard things so astounding that they cannot be expressed in words, things no human is allowed to tell. 2 Corinthians 12: 1- 4

It is erroneously taught by some that when we die our spirits are asleep.

The body is what disintegrates from the curse resulted upon the earth due to Adam's sin, however the soul never dies it is eternal.

One's spirit is forever conscious.

When we perish within body our soul will exist fully alive.

If one is a Christian/follower/saved believer in God their spirit will move directly from the body at the moment of death into the presence of the Lord Jesus until his "second coming".

Afterwards we who are in Christ will receive brand new resurrected bodies to house us as we live forever on the new earth with God.

If one is an unbeliever the destination for their spirit is the immediate entrance into Hades- a place for the wicked after death.

The unbelievers will reside there until the "second death" in which they will be thrown into the lake if fire.

And I saw a great white throne and the one sitting on it. The earth and sky fled from his presence, but they found no place to hide.

I saw the dead, both great and small, standing before God's throne. And the books were opened, including the Book of Life.

And the dead were judged according to what they had done, as recorded in the books. The sea gave up its dead, and death and the grave gave up their dead.

And all were judged according to their deeds. Then death and the grave were thrown into the lake of fire.

This lake of fire is the second death. And anyone whose name was not found recorded in the Book of Life was thrown into the lake of fire.- Revelation 20: 11-15

Jesus said, "There was a certain rich man who was splendidly clothed in purple and fine linen and who lived each day in luxury. At his gate lay a poor man named Lazarus who was covered with sores.

As Lazarus lay there longing for scraps from the rich man's table, the dogs would come and lick his open sores.

"Finally, the poor man died and was carried by the angels to sit beside Abraham at the heavenly banquet. The rich man also died and was buried, and he went to the place of the dead.

There, in torment, he saw Abraham in the far distance with Lazarus at his side.

"The rich man shouted, 'Father Abraham, have some pity! Send Lazarus over here to dip the tip of his finger in water and cool my tongue. I am in anguish in these flames.'

"But Abraham said to him, 'Son, remember that during your lifetime you had everything you wanted, and Lazarus had nothing.

So now he is here being comforted, and you are in anguish. And besides, there is a great chasm separating us.

No one can cross over to you from here, and no one can cross over to us from there.'

"Then the rich man said, 'Please, Father Abraham, at least send him to my father's home. For I have five brothers, and I want *him to warn them so they don't end up in this place of torment.'*

'But Abraham said, 'Moses and the prophets have warned them.

Your brothers can read what they wrote.'

'The rich man replied, 'No, Father Abraham! But if someone is sent to them from the dead, then they will repent of their sins and turn to God.'

'But Abraham said, 'If they won't listen to Moses and the prophets, they won't be persuaded even if someone rises from the dead.'" Luke 16: 19-31

* * *

Paradise

There are the terms people speak or phrase verbally such as "Heaven on earth" or "Living in paradise".

A luxury vacation in a beautiful location overseas or within other states can be a person's example of experiencing their sense of "heaven on earth".

An environment where one lives rich or famously in a predicament where they seemingly have the world at their feet with all that money can buy.

This may be a pleasure and satisfaction for many, but it is nowhere near the definition of what true paradise or heaven on earth is.

There is absolutely nothing wrong with enjoying the scenery and experience of nature within the essences of recreation, leisure, and exploration gorgeously.

These encounters are temporary.

They are also lacking within perfection and certainty.

Aside from everything having their potential flaws, these fancy and wonderful places or situations can all be destroyed within an instant by unforeseen events.

A natural disaster is just one example as something to possibly occur to tarnish or bring a setback to one's so-called heaven or paradise.

When Jesus returns to earth, he will raise all of our deceased bodies that have decayed to be reunited with each of our living souls.

Our bodies will be renewed, perfected, and significant- though distinct- within identification to the bodies that we currently inhabit now.

We will permanently reside in a place/setting similar in resemblance to the present world we live in now.

*That is what the Scriptures mean when they say, "No eye has seen, no ear has heard, and no mind has imagined what God has prepared for those who love him." **1 Corinthians 2:9***

The current heaven is an ethereal state where when the spirits of us believers separate from the body at physical death enter immediately into the presence of God.

In spite of this fact, this is not our final destination. It is just the intermediate state of being- an advancement in the process of made perfect in holiness befitting us for the presence of God.

Four

Relationship

⚜

A Very Best Friend

I had always considered my mother and my deceased dog "Brandie" of seventeen years to have been two of my very best friends here on the entire planet.

There is another friend I have come to know as a best friend.

One who sticks closer to me than any other ever could or would.

I had known him for years, ever since I was a child, but did not know or realize the depth of the relationship that had developed between us.

While I had often misinterpreted and misunderstand this individual and his character he ultimately interpreted and understood me, and was always very patient and compassionate toward me when I did not even recognize it.

This individual gave me my space to discover, learn and to grow through each of my circumstances and situations.

Though he gave me room to figure out things, he was always near within reach, never to leave me out from his presence.

Now that my eyes are open to see clearer, my mind is receptive to the fact that the friend I once thought of as indifferent outside of me, was actually the constant companion who lived ever so benevolently inside of me.

This friend's name is Jesus and he literally lives inside of me and he is not going away because he promised not to.

And, this friend of mine, unlike others, does not tell any lies.

So, if he makes any type of statement, I can definitely rely on whatever claim is made by him.

Jesus is a very good friend of mine who loves me more than my mother or dog, or anyone else is capable of loving and caring for me, and that is phenomenal.

He is there for me at any moment of the day when I need or want to talk.

There is never a time when he is unavailable or not in the mood to hear or listen to my voice and concerns.

He carries me when I am unable to walk and he holds me up when I feel like I am going to fall.

He knows me better than I know myself and he knows where to lead me when I don't know where to go.

I can depend on him and I do.

I surrender to Jesus because I want him to lead me and guide me through life.

As a true friend who has the extraordinary heart of a parent and beloved pet who both love unconditionally, I know that I can entrust my entire being into his supervision and care.

Oh, what a wonderful friend that I have in my Lord Jesus, one who is genuine and true. A very best friend to the end-which in return will be my true new beginning.

* * *

Living For The Lord

I always believed in you.

Then, I accepted you as my Lord and Savior at the age between ten or twelve.

I went through some hardships that sometimes made me doubt you.

I even separated myself from you for a while out of anger, and misunderstanding of your nature.

Nonetheless, the essence of your spirit still produced a purity within me.

Through it all, everything turned out okay.

You taught me so much. You gave to me so much. You cared for me so much.

Upon my reunion with you, I gave myself completely to you. Never to depart from you, never to go astray. I am not meant to be that way.

I wake up in delight of your presence, I spend the day talking to you, walking in your grace.

I retire in the night with you, drifting off to sleep under your guard.

The words I read in scripture bring life into meaning. They bring food to my soul, power into my spirit.

I do not live life on my own, I have really grown. I have never been of this world; I am not of it. I do not want any part of it.

I live my life for you, because of you. You live through me; you are within me.

You created me to have a relationship with you, to get totally acquainted with you.

This partnership is supernatural, very extraordinary of its kind.

A companionship to treasure, and one that will last forever.

* * *

The Lord's hold On Me: I Belong To God

I did not ask to come into this world. I did not have any say so within the matter.

All I can do is trust in the Lord and what he has planned.

He intended my purpose before I was created, he will fulfill his aim to when I become designated.

My life is not my own It belongs to God. He chose me as one of his very own long before the foundation of the world.

The Lord already knew all about me, he designed me.

What I had to go through to where I am at now was determined before I could understand how the application of my exploration would give me a better understanding of my true dedication.

A chance to get to know God better, a chance to realize how blessed I have been, a chance to appreciate the providence and protection that has constantly been over me.

The Lord, who refused to let me go.

The Lord, who knew I did not know the true love that he endeavored to show.

The Lord, who from him, many gifts to me he bestowed.

Through a sudden and tragic unspoken fear, he readily triumphed to draw me near, replacing that fear with trust and hope, something that became an absolute must.

No God, you did not deal harshly with me, now only I can see.

You returned to me the memories of the past to fast forward to me the present unto the future, to assure and confirm to me that you will continue to do everything you promised to do.

Thank you.

* * *

Spending Time With God: The Power Of The Lord

The name of the Lord is very powerful. When I call on the name Jesus he never fails to come.

The devil will run instantly at the sound of his name. Peace will come immediately by the faith in his name.

I have experienced these realities all too personally and can readily, boldly, and joyfully give testimony to each and every tale of power that came from the result of believing and acting on the name of Jesus Christ.

In the morning, evening, and afternoon I consult with the Lord.

I speak to him even if it is just to say, "Hi".

I tell God how I feel, ask him what he thinks about things I am unsure of, or I just explain to him how I feel.

The Lord does not ignore me either because I seek him with all of my heart.

God knows our true intentions.

He often answers me in a number of ways. One fashion is through my thoughts.

As one of the Lord's sheep, I do know his voice and I listen to him.

The closer we are to God the deeper he reveals and displays himself to us and significantly within our lives.

It is wonderful to know that we can turn to the Lord for any and everything.

He is consistent and will not waver in providing for all our essential needs and humble desires.

It brings me great comfort to immerse myself in God's word when I read through scripture and biblically inspired content.

It enlivens the holy spirit within me, giving a literal warmth, and consoling grasp to my body.

I feel a nice soothe from the spirit. A connection in harmony with being fed wholesome.

The best meal to taste is the one where we consume the word of the Lord.

I eat and drink of it relaxed in bed, spending moments or even hours sometimes earnestly gathering instruction and knowledge before going to sleep.

Engaging in a relationship with God brings such fulfillment and a greater hope.

Five

Insight

Discernment

Last night, the pastor of the church I attended since September came into my mind. I thought about the settling that remained within my spirit after heeding the warning about him.

I still felt that stillness.

It wasn't until I watched two of his latest sermons online that my spirit became rattled once again.

Just by watching and listening to him those feelings came back. Those enlightening inclinations about him.

Those same vibes of caution, but now even stronger.

The words he preached even gave details and glimpses into the true reveal of his disposition.

I think confronting him on the issue that I had with him brought out the truth of his conscious as he admitted his guilt on a few things in front of the congregation.

I noticed it because I knew what was partly behind his address.

He confessed how he struggled with being completely honest within his forthcoming with people, and how he needed to work on specific things within his nature and character.

From his own mouth he acknowledged that he was resentful at times and had anger, hurt, and disappointment when his flaws were honestly pointed out.

This was only half of the story to my full discernment.

One of my strongest gifts from the Lord is sensing things about people in areas that others cannot sense or pick up right away.

I am not at all being judgmental on this man.

Nonetheless, God will make known unto us what he wants us to pay attention to and be secured against.

The Lord is just reminding and reaffirming to me that just because someone is a leader within the church does not mean they are perfect or the ultimate example of a fully mature Christian.

Many battle inwardly as they too are only human.

Some are more troubled or incorrect than others.

Either way, I know this pastor is someone for me to stay away from.

The statements from my inner voice of spirited repeated again from the recent past, "He cannot be trusted, he is trouble, stay away from him".

The message pierced right threw, giving me a bad feeling, a feeling I have received within the past when I was being supernaturally informed through intuition and gut feelings to beware of someone, a condition, or situation.

I am thankful to God for his divine guidance and instruction, even if or when others in particular are unable to decipher.

The Lord interacts with us all differently as we are all unique in design.

I had planned to eventually visit the church again on a regular basis when able, however, after last night, I don't see that happening.

It is not at all that I am letting the pastor's negativity keep me away from Sunday worship because I was going to go regardless beforehand.

I never let other people's insecurity, hang up, pretense, or ignorance deter me.

However, some elements play a larger role in the events that take place and I will move on to another church the Lord will lead me to when the time is right.

Things enter our lives not always to take place as a permanent residence, but as a stepping stone to another more prominent built or structured abode.

* * *

Messages From The Lord: Childhood Memories

When I was around nine years of age, I remember a piercing dream that I had at the time.

I was an extremely sensitive (very intuitive/spiritually inclined) child back then, keenly intelligent and highly aware. I was in-tuned to my surroundings whether physical or spiritual.

This was no ordinary dream; within the vision my mother had passed away and I was at her graveside burial.

The idea of my mother dying or being dead at that early time in my life was both heartbreaking and earth-shattering.

Yes, quite traumatic and momentous. I could not have imagined life without her.

It would have destroyed me so young because I loved her tremendously and we had a special bond.

In the morning, when I awoke from the dream, the emotional residue from what I had encountered lingered with me a bit.

Soon I realized that my mother was not actually going to die, however, I was being divinely guided with discipline.

God was using a devastating example to teach me a very valuable lesson.

The training behind the reprimand was to have more appreciation for my mother.

The Lord's act was warranted, and even at that age of nine it was appropriate and I understood.

There were times when I was not being considerate and showing an unjustifiable attitude toward my mom due to whatever was going on within me.

I told my mother about the dream afterwards because I shared everything with her.

She agreed with me about the message I received.

I took the instruction from God appreciatively as I appreciated the warning and I indeed appreciated my mom all the more.

The Lord's correction was done purely out his righteousness, and for his abundant love and compassion for my mother.

I am so grateful that he also loved me enough to discipline me and show me where I was wrong.

God used a significant tactic, the projection of how precious it was to respect and to value the presence of my mother in my life.

My mother had informed to me later in life that she prayed to the Lord when I was a baby to allow her to live long enough to see me able to become an adult, able to take care of myself.

She didn't ever want me to be mistreated or without the necessities of survival just like any exceptional mother who would lay down their life for their child would not.

God generously granted my mother her request and gave us very long years together. She was able to see me fend for myself, and her too, within the process.

I am thankful to the Lord for giving me enough wonderful time with such a dear and loving mother.

There are so many in life who didn't get the chance or opportunity to grow up with a parent due to losing them early on in life.

My heart goes out to all who have experienced this unfortunate circumstance in life.

It is important to treasure what matters most within our lives and live each day within recognition of each blessing.

Six

Holy Spirit

When I was a child, I spoke and thought and reasoned as a child. But when I grew up, I put away childish things. -1 Corinthians 13:11

I remember during my twenties I was very strong in prayer and talking to God, and getting feedback from the Lord.

Although he stays the same within his character situations do incline to change depending on our behavior, growth, trial, outlook, and so on.

Many factors can play a role in our relationship with God.

I've noticed through various stages of my life from childhood to adulthood the different ways I'd feel the Lord's presence and recognized his footprints making an impact.

He was always there but incorporated his provision in a wide range of demonstration according to how I progressed, and spiritually matured.

For example, when a baby is weaned off the bottle and can begin to eat solid food, they soon learn to balance drink with a cup and thoroughly chew with their teeth.

The baby is starting to develop into a state where the parent doesn't have to feed them as an infant needs to be fed anymore.

Like newborn babies, you must crave pure spiritual milk so that you will grow into a full experience of salvation. Cry out for this nourishment, now that you have had a taste of the Lord's kindness. -1 Peter 2:2-3

The child is becoming capable of feeding them self with the nurturing beforehand of the parent and the maturing of the body.

Eventually the child will walk on its own, talk, use the toilet on its own and then start school.

So, the child will still need their parent's guidance and supervision, however, the parent no longer has to carry the child in the way they did before.

Let your roots grow down into him, and let your lives be built on him. Then your faith will grow strong in the truth you were taught, and you will overflow with thankfulness. -Colossians 2:7

Once we get to the levels where we need to be there are higher steps in experiencing the way God can and does work in our lives.

He deals with us at our own pace he meets us where we're at he knows if we are ready or not to move forward in certain areas and how we'll be responsive.

Our experiences teach us, strengthen us, and enable us to deepen our relationship with the Lord if we allow our hearts to be directed through him.

Even when we don't willingly desire to go through the bad times (and who does) he brings us out of our circumstances as better people. We then notice and hear his voice in an array of discerning ways.

Consider it pure joy, my brothers and sisters, whenever you face trials of many kinds, because you know that the testing of your faith produces perseverance. Let perseverance finish its work so that you may be mature and complete, not lacking anything. -James 1:2-4

And I am certain that God, who began the good work within you, will continue his work until it is finally finished on the day when Christ Jesus returns. -Philippians 1:6

* * *

Do you have the gift of speaking? Then speak as though God himself were speaking through you.

Do you have the gift of helping others?

Do it with all the strength and energy that God supplies. Then everything you do will bring glory to God through Jesus Christ. All glory and power to him forever and ever! Amen. 1 Peter 4:11

Sometimes God will speak directly to us through certain people to communicate to us exactly what he may want us to know.

He may have an encouraging word to share, a message of hope.

He may also take it upon himself to bring a little clarity and comfort to a situation one may have been struggling with.

The Lord goes these extra steps to show us just how much he loves us and to express his total concern for our well-being.

We will recognize when our Lord is corresponding with us by knowing his voice even if it is spoken by a human tongue.

A feeling of ease, peace, or contentment will settle around our presence, and upon the circumstance that has troubled or affected one.

This is what happened to me-someone else's experience may be different.

In addition, the Lord stayed up with me all night (not that he ever sleeps) keeping me company and helping me to write as he worked his power through me to utilize my talents for his glory.

I am so impressed by God.

My literature just flowed out effortlessly; I wasn't even expecting it because earlier in the day I had wanted to write but did not feel up to it.

I was feeling kind of down about something, but he just came and lifted up my spirits and kept me in place- holding me nearby.

The Lord even had gotten me excited in the process.

And when I read his word in certain parts of scripture, I just love the way he talks and how he tells it like it is with such feeling and vigor.

God is something else! But most of all he is my confidant- my everything!

To one person the Spirit gives the ability to give wise advice; to another the same Spirit gives a message of special knowledge.

The same Spirit gives great faith to another, and to someone else the one Spirit gives the gift of healing.

He gives one person the power to perform miracles, and another the ability to prophesy.

He gives someone else the ability to discern whether a message is from the Spirit of God or from another spirit.

Still another person is given the ability to speak in unknown languages, while another is given the ability to interpret what is being said. 1 Corinthians 12:8-10

* * *

The Best Worst Day Of Your Life

You can make many plans, but the Lords purpose will prevail. -Proverbs 19:21

Have you ever been rudely left at the altar, had an explosive argument just before the wedding that prevented the ceremony from taking place, or decided to say "I do not instead of I do" to the bride or groom in response to the minister who recited the agreement of the sacred vows in front of a gathering of invited guests?

Well, if so, consider the incident a blessing in disguise.

All situations that do not go as planned or that may turn out as unfortunate events are sometimes actually put into occurrence to help and not to hurt.

There are distinct warnings, signs, or gut feelings that the holy spirit imparts to us that we may overlook, dismiss, or not take full notice of then either learn from or regret later on from our failure to heed insight.

Messages can even be spoken through another person in relation to one's particular circumstance.

We just have to be careful and test the information to make sure the advice and input is indeed a source from the spirit.

Those who are like me, strong within the gift of discernment would know immediately or familiarly when truth and essence is being told or spoken.

Any type of hint that is rooted in our experience and inner-knowing comes naturally by the ability to recognize where it is originating from.

There have been people who have known better about something yet went into a condition anyway. Many of us have did things against our better judgment.

However, why enter into mishap, or error when it can be avoided, especially when alerted by divine intervention?

I know there are times when I look back on certain life wants that didn't go well or as hoped for to later really appreciate that the circumstance saved me from an unpleasant or undesirable outcome.

There were other preferable steps I was motioned toward that brought about greater encounters and expectations.

So, when God says no or not yet, it is because the request or situation is not meant or not ready to go into effect.

God's timing is different from ours he knows just when to deliver what is best.

A "no" answer is often a surprise that leads to a greater event than you could never have imagined possible as a follow up, and suitable conclusion.

Thank our good Lord for the particular happenings that go wrong in order to show us in the direction of the things that will go right.

The LORD will work out his plans for my life— for your faithful love, O LORD, endures forever. Don't abandon me, for you made me. -Psalms 138:8

Seven

Sex

All of us are different we all have our own needs, preferences, and desires.

I have never been into sex and do not have any lustful urges or attraction for men or women.

I am not and never have been a lesbian nor have I ever been in a heterosexual love relationship.

I just do not have any of those type of feelings, and pleasantly so.

Yes, God created sexual intercourse and intimacy between a man and a woman and there is nothing wrong with these emotions being expressed in its proper context as the Lord intended.

However, there is no commandment or sin in not wanting to engage within a romantic relationship.

I never had a need or yearning for a boyfriend or a marriage partner.

I did not care what direction the world was headed into because I was never a follower of the popular culture.

I was not afraid to stand out even if I was misunderstood, ridiculed, mocked, or targeted from being considered unusual.

I was more concerned with the peace and purity within spirit.

I am not defined by what I do and do not do with my body, but I am identified by the spirit within me that inspires what I do and do not do with the temple that I live in.

My circumstance feels completely natural and suitable to the individual that I am.

The spirit has brought to me a peace, comfort, and joy unlike no other.

There are undoubtedly times that are hard, life is not easy. Even though, God is there, he permeates through the negativity to rejuvenate the positivity.

Let that power shine, and rest abundantly in the light that

sustains.

* * *

Unwed

I knew ever since childhood that I would never grow up to get married.

The desire was never within my heart.

I didn't even want to have a boyfriend. I still don't, and I never will.

I don't believe that marriage and intimate sexual relationship is for everybody.

I do believe as I always have that there are men who don't have sex until they are married and men who don't- and have never cheated on their wives.

Some may believe that is a naive view to hold, but in reality, it is not.

The majority of men may not fit into this category, though, there are far too many men in the world for them all to be sexually promiscuous and cheaters.

People seek out marriage for many different reasons depending on culture and personal values.

I just never saw a purpose for the undertaking in my life.

I never felt the need for a man to make me happy. I never believed happiness came from a man.

I always found happiness from within my spirit.

I never felt the need for a man to complete me (which I don't understand the void in certain women who do feel this way.) I naturally felt whole and complete within myself as an individual.

I've never even understood the concept of falling in love with a man.

I've fell in love with a puppy before, but never a man.

I don't have those feelings or sexual desires and I am perfectly happy that way.

When I read in the bible as a youngster of Paul's statements in regard to it being "**better not to marry**" in 1 Corinthians 7:40 I could identify with his words and considered it a gift indeed to not have any sexual or romantic need.

In a world where I was considered not normal for not wanting to get married or to have sex, I was proud and unbothered.

Yes, each of you should remain as you were when God called you.

God paid a high price for you, so don't be enslaved by the world. Each of you, dear brothers and sisters, should remain as you were when God first called you.

Now regarding your question about the young women who are not yet married. I do not have a command from the Lord for them.

But the Lord in his mercy has given me wisdom that can be trusted, and I will share it with you. Because of the present crisis, I think it is best to remain as you are.

I want you to be free from the concerns of this life. An unmarried man can spend his time doing the Lord's work and thinking how to please him.

But a married man has to think about his earthly responsibilities and how to please his wife. His interests are divided.

In the same way, a woman who is no longer married or has never been married can be devoted to the Lord and holy in body and in spirit.

But a married woman has to think about her earthly responsibilities and how to please her husband.

I am saying this for your benefit, not to place restrictions on you.

I want you to do whatever will help you serve the Lord best, with as few distractions as possible.

But in my opinion it would be better for her to stay single, and I think I am giving you counsel from God's Spirit when I say this. - 1 Corinthians 7:20-40

Yes, and also as a woman, and a human being, I am so glad that not having a desire for marriage is not a sin.

If I was interested, I would have had a very hard time obeying any man and having him as head over me within my personal life.

I was never the subservient type and too independent.

I enjoy the single life where I am just fully committed and aligned with being fully obedient to God.

* * *

Sin

At that moment their eyes were opened, and they suddenly felt shame at their nakedness.

So they sewed fig leaves together to cover themselves.

When the cool evening breezes were blowing, the man and his wife heard the LORD God walking about in the garden.

So they hid from the LORD God among the trees.

Then the LORD God called to the man, "Where are you?"

He replied, "I heard you walking in the garden, so I hid. I was afraid because I was naked."

"Who told you that you were naked?" the LORD God asked. "Have you eaten from the tree whose fruit I commanded you not to eat?" -Genesis 3:7-11

And to the man he said, "Since you listened to your wife and ate from the tree whose fruit I commanded you not to eat, the ground is cursed because of you.

All your life you will struggle to scratch a living from it. -Genesis 3:17

Sin is a reproach to God. It goes against everything that he is.

God is not only love, but God is holy.

God cannot tolerate anything unjust or corrupt.

When he tells us not to sin it is for our own good and not to harm us or keep us from enjoyment.

It is sometimes so hard for us to break away from certain sins of the world because we were born into error and it is natural for us to be incline to what is inherently familiar to our environment and surroundings.

In our lives we've done things we didn't even recognize or think of as sin because of our innate proneness.

Whether one struggles with anger, selfishness, pride, hate, envy, jealousy, lying, stealing, gossiping and etc....

Our Lord in heaven understands our shortcomings and inability to uphold to his standards. He does not condemn us he wants to help each and every one of us who call out to him.

God knows there are things we cannot do on our own and that we need his holy spirit to enable us to be more like Christ.

Everyone is an individual with their own different set of circumstances or personal battles. No one is the same and we all have distinct ways of looking at things, and ways of feeling about things.

So, no one should go around to assume what is going on with a person, what they are going through, and/or why.

God does not want us to carry the heavy load of stress, guilt, unworthiness, depression, sadness or anything else disheartening we are to lay all of our burdens, cares and worries on him. Then we must trust in him enough to see us through.

It is not possible for us to do anything without God. Only with God are all things possible!

* * *

Food For Thought
Can You Trust Your Spouse?

My mother told me a story years ago about an article she had read in a Watchtower magazine left behind by a Jehovah's witness.

In the story, there was a woman who remained a virgin until marriage.

She eventually conceived her very first child, and everything turned out okay.

The woman then sometime later gave birth to her second child, and everything was okay.

After the woman delivered a third baby throughout the marriage, she discovered that she was infected with the HIV/AIDS virus.

Her husband had given her this life-threatening deadly disease from either being unfaithful during their union or from carrying it all along until finally it manifested unto his wife, or both.

But the man who commits adultery is an utter fool, for he destroys himself. -Proverbs 6:32

Give honor to marriage, and remain faithful to one another in marriage. God will surely judge people who are immoral and those who commit adultery. -Hebrews 13:4

* * *

Can You Trust Who You Are Dating?

This is what the LORD says: "Cursed are those who put their trust in mere humans, who rely on human strength and turn their hearts away from the LORD. -Jeremiah 17:5

"The human heart is the most deceitful of all things, and desperately wicked. Who really knows how bad it is?

But I, the LORD, search all hearts and examine secret motives. I give all people their due rewards, according to what their actions deserve." -Jeremiah 17:9-10

I loved to read ever since I was a youngster. My mother used to buy me different kinds of books all the time whenever I was interested in something.

She'd even bring me literature as she thought of me while she would be out running on an errand here and there.

This was one of the things my mother loved about me- my knowledge, my quest for knowledge, and my discernment.

It is also something I loved very much about my mother too.

She was a very smart and intelligent woman for all the years I had grown up with her.

As a teen, I read quite a few magazines out of curiosity and to keep up with my observant nature.

Although I wasn't a part of the world spiritually, I was aware of everything around me and of what was going on in the world. God had blessed me that way.

Even though I did not live my life within the tendency of mainstream society and was not inspired by what motivated the majority It did not stop me from delving into the pages and media of various lifestyles and experiences.

I think I was about fourteen or fifteen when I read an article in "Seventeen" magazine.

The story was about a teenager who had contracted the herpes virus. I do not remember every detail word for word but I do recall very clearly the situation.

The girl was ashamed, consumed with guilt, and worried about how to tell her boyfriend about her venereal disease.

So, one day she came out and told him and he responded in a way she did not expect.

Her boyfriend told her something like, "Don't worry about it. It's okay, I still love you.

The teen was surprised and felt relieved that her boyfriend was understanding of her circumstance.

To have possibly spread herpes to him through contracting the virus from a past relationship to how he would react to her revealing this information to him was pure torture for her.

As some time passed, the teen girl had one day visited her boyfriend and looked into the medicine cabinet of his bathroom when she spotted a prescription bottle.

The bottle had been prescribed for her boyfriend in the treatment of the herpes virus. This is the moment by a chance encounter that she discovered it was him who had given her the disease to begin with.

Her boyfriend knew all along that he had genital herpes.

Yet, he pretended, and allowed his girlfriend to believe she put him at risk when he was the one to pass it on to her.

I read from the pages of books, viewed from the scenes of media, and even witnessed from people all around me the deep/heavy accounts of what unfavorably touched their lives at an early age.

It played a part in my forewarning of the world, and just how contaminated it really is.

God speaks to us within so many ways to alert, teach, guide, and protect his children from the vile lures and traps of society.

But as for your gods, see if you can find them, and let the person who has taken them die! And if you find anything else that belongs to you, identify it before all these relatives of ours, and I will give it back!"

But Jacob did not know that Rachel had stolen the household idols. -Genesis 31:32

Laban went first into Jacob's tent to search there, then into Leah's, and then the tents of the two servant wives—but he found nothing.

Finally, he went into Rachel's tent. But Rachel had taken the household idols and hidden them in her camel saddle, and now she was sitting on them.

When Laban had thoroughly searched her tent without finding them, she said to her father, "Please, sir, forgive me if I don't get up for you. I'm having my monthly period."

So Laban continued his search, but he could not find the household idols. Genesis 31:33-35

* * *

Abortion And Immorality In Marriage And Out Of Wedlock

Then Jesus stood up again and said to the woman, "Where are your accusers? Didn't even one of them condemn you?"

"No, Lord," she said. And Jesus said,

"Neither do I. Go and sin no more." -John 8:10-11

A lot of people blame the reason for abortion on the result of immoral behavior such as fornication/premarital sex when indeed this is not always the case or the primary desire, remedy, or conclusion that everyone comes to.

There are wanted pregnancies outside of marriage and there are unwanted pregnancies inside of marriage, and I know for a fact there are plenty of married couples who opted for the convenience of having an abortion to terminate a pregnancy.

I personally knew married people who aborted more than one child throughout their marriage.

Everybody cannot be generalized and scooped up into one category.

Society has a habit of putting people into a widely held, fixed and oversimplified image or idea of what particular types of situations, individuals and things represent.

Marriage itself is not a safe haven for morality or justification when it focuses on sex, reproduction, and parenting.

There are people who get married for financial security, social status, or out of a feeling of obligation whether personal or religious.

Not everyone marries out of true love and to enter into a sacred commitment.

Some even have open marriages with multiple sexual partners.

Give honor to marriage, and remain faithful to one another in marriage. God will surely judge people who are immoral and those who commit adultery. -Hebrews 13;4

There are single parents who raise their children up in better homes, or whose children turn out finer than those within a two-parent home, I know, I lovingly came from a one parent home- living with my mother's side of the family- and I would not have changed the circumstance for the world because every man is not cut out to be a father, and vice versa.

There were grown men who were jealous and resentful of me because their daughters and sons were out running wild and uncontrollably while I was the total opposite- not at all conformed to the ways of the world.

I had a very good mother who was spiritual and blessed by God and we were both lead by the spirit.

This is a fallen world (so certain nontraditional as well as unfortunate things do and will happen) yet illegitimate children are not dismissed or unloved by God and neither or those who may have had children out of wedlock. ***Children are a gift from the LORD; they are a reward from him. -Psalms 127:3***

God knows everyone's situation and he knows their heart.

A lot of people judge on what they do not know or see as God sees all- knowing our true conditions, regards and intentions.

So don't make judgments about anyone ahead of time—before

the Lord returns. For he will bring our darkest secrets to light and will reveal our private motives. Then God will give to each one whatever praise is due. -1 Corinthians 4:5

"Do not judge others, and you will not be judged. For you will be treated as you treat others. The standard you use in judging is the standard by which you will be judged.

"And why worry about a speck in your friend's eye when you have a log in your own? How can you think of saying to your friend, 'Let me help you get rid of that speck in your eye,' when you can't see past the log in your own eye?

Hypocrite! First get rid of the log in your own eye; then you will see well enough to deal with the speck in your friend's eye. -Matthew 7:1-5

All unwed mothers or even fathers are not promiscuous or unrighteous.

Some women get raped, deceived, or are just unconventional within distinction.

The same goes with men, they may get misled, seduced or they too may have their own distinct mindset.

When my mother got pregnant with me my father told her to get an abortion.

She refused his suggestion because she wanted me -not him (she was not looking or depending on my father to help her take care of me)- and she was not at all ashamed when she had me.

My grandfather (my mother's father) completely supported her decision to have me and told her "I am glad you want to keep your baby", and he was a very gifted and intelligent man who believed in God.

This article is in no way promoting fornication/premarital sex or glorifying childbirth to unmarried people.

What I am laying out as a fact is that marriage is not the solution to preventing abortion and sex outside of wedlock is not the genuine culprit resulting in many abortions.

It is all about listening to God and putting him first.

If individuals honored God in everything they did or at least made an effort to then these issues would be less of a major problem and burden within society.

A marriage between individuals lead by God would be in genuine love, respect, partnership, faith and obedience to the Lord.

Therefore, the event of an abortion would not exist upon the conception of an unplanned, unexpected, or possible inconvenient arrival of a child (due to financial or other setbacks and limitations), however, when decisions are based on one's own lack of faith and/or followed by one's own way and selfish desire this is where things tend to go wrong.

Commendably, we do have believers in the world who are the prime examples of a wonderful adoring God-blessed union.

Everybody encounters their own troubles and problems, but for the most part their life is spiritually finer within contribute to the Lord's presence. *"Now therefore, O sons, listen to me, For blessed are they who keep my ways. -Proverbs 8:32*

The same goes for single people.

It is not the fornication and unwanted pregnancy that results in abortion.

It is not taking heed to what the Lord instructs on how to live and conduct our lives.

If the entire world adhered to God's principles there would be no sexual immorality or abortions.

There are plenty of things we do not agree with or want in this world and present life, yet we still must yield to the word of God instead of what we may deem as suitable, regardless of how unfair or not right it may seem to us. *Trust in the LORD with all your heart; do not depend on your own understanding. Seek his will in all you do, and he will show you which path to take. -Proverbs 3:5-6*

If you need wisdom, ask our generous God, and he will give it to you. He will not rebuke you for asking. -James 1:5

Listen to the Lord, and not to man's self-serving and deceitful interpretation of what the bible directs.

And now I make one more appeal, my dear brothers and sisters.

Watch out for people who cause divisions and upset people's faith by teaching things contrary to what you have been taught.

Stay away from them. Such people are not serving Christ our Lord; they are serving their own personal interests.

By smooth talk and glowing words they deceive innocent people. -Romans 16:17-18

For a time is coming when people will no longer listen to sound and wholesome teaching.

They will follow their own desires and will look for teachers who will tell them whatever their itching ears want to hear. -2 Timothy 4:3

God does not give out specific rules to us to withhold, limit, or to destroy our contentment and well being.

It is the mere opposite.

His guidance is to protect, preserve, and maintain our wellness through the wisdom and knowledge that we are unable to grasp within his solicitous attention and care for us.

Satan seeks to steal away all that God originally had planned for us because he has a vendetta against the Lord.

We are just tools in his scheme to build against God to tear up the beauty that he constructed by puncturing out the image of his creation.

Satan is a liar, a thief and a murderer.

He wants to take as many people to hell with him as possible. Don't let him manipulate or persuade you.

Turn and go to Jesus who sets all things straight and right. He is the truth, a giver, a healer and a restorer.

God is not anxious to condemn you for your errors he is eager to save and to redeem you from them altogether!

The Lord isn't really being slow about his promise, as some people think. No, he is being patient for your sake. He does not want anyone to be destroyed, but wants everyone to repent. -2 Peter 3:9

The Lord earnestly desires for you to come to know him so that he can teach you the truth in how to walk correctly in this life so that you will walk perfectly within the next.

Give your life to Jesus, he will never abort you!

Those who know your name trust in you, for you, O LORD, do not abandon those who search for you. -Psalms 9:10

Now may the God of peace make you holy in every way, and may your whole spirit and soul and body be kept blameless until our Lord Jesus Christ comes again. 1 Thessalonians 5:23

Eight

Opened Arms

Nothing Is Hidden From God

Oh, how great are God's riches and wisdom and knowledge! How impossible it is for us to understand his decisions and his ways! For who can know the Lord's thoughts?

Who knows enough to give him advice? -Romans 11:33-34

I never understood the idea or concept of those who sought to keep their thoughts and actions hidden from God.

No matter what perception we had of God- the loving, merciful one or the angry, vengeful one- I was never disappointed in the fact the he was aware of our every thought, feeling, and action.

If anything, I was glad about this advantage of his.

An advantage that some of us even share a touch of within certain spiritual gifts that God anoints some of us with.

As sovereign, we as a people need one who knows all and sees all, especially living among a fallen world where people tend to judge by what is on the outside as well as by only what they sometimes want to see.

Our God sees the absolute truth inside each and every one of us. He knows our true motives and what lies within our hearts.

Unlike others who jump to conclusions without gathering up all or enough information, who form an opinion prematurely based on a false perception, and who take out of context what is not comprehended, God already holds the full spectrum accurately and ultimately on point.

He knows us far better than we know ourselves and we need a ruler just as himself to make things right.

If all was left to mankind on their own to decide the final word, we'd all be in trouble- worse trouble than what the world is in now.

So for those in particular who are concerned about what God knows about their sin, instead of looking to hide look to admit and to repent and learn to appreciate that we have a God that looks to forgive.

But it was to us that God revealed these things by his Spirit. For his Spirit searches out everything and shows us God's deep secrets. No one can know a person's thoughts except that person's own spirit, and no one can know God's thoughts except God's own Spirit. -1 Corinthians 2:10-11

* * *

Too Sullied To Be Saved?

From the depths of despair, O LORD, I call for your help.

Hear my cry, O Lord. Pay attention to my prayer.

LORD, if you kept a record of our sins, who, O Lord, could ever survive? But you offer forgiveness, that we might learn to fear you.

I am counting on the LORD; yes, I am counting on him. I have put my hope in his word. -Psalms 130:1-5

There are people who believe that they have done far too many terrible things in life for God to forgive and save them.

Out of extreme shame, guilt and sorrow over their mistakes these people conclude God would never sympathize or accept them.

The taunting and haunting residue from past or present deeds, inspire them to feel doomed.

They imagine the worse possible outcome and are left to feel unworthy to come to God as they expect nothing but his severe wrath and punishment.

Many of these people beat themselves up over and over again struck by memory after memory then tortured by fear and a sense of being lost with no kind of hope.

However, God/Jesus wants to erase those bad reflections. He wants to stop that self-abuse. He wants to heal that pain.

He wants to exchange wrath and punishment for grace and mercy. He wants to offer a wonderful end result.

He wants to replace mental anguish with peace. He wants to pour out his love.

He wants to recruit into his family.

He wants to cleanse and purify to make a new.

He wants to eradicate false belief- so that true belief is in him.

There is no greater example than of the story of Saul/Paul in the bible. He was "a chief of sin" yet overcame by the favor and power of the Lord.

In Paul's wicked days he persecuted and murdered Christians but God had an incredible conversion ahead for this man who became one of the most beloved disciples of Jesus Christ.

But God had mercy on me so that Christ Jesus could use me as a prime example of his great patience with even the worst sinners. Then others will realize that they, too, can believe in him and receive eternal life. -1 Timothy 1:16

You know what I was like when I followed the Jewish religion—how I violently persecuted God's church. I did my best to destroy it. I was far ahead of my fellow Jews in my zeal for the traditions of my ancestors.

But even before I was born, God chose me and called me by his marvelous grace. Then it pleased him to reveal his Son to me so that I would proclaim the Good News about Jesus to the Gentiles. When this happened, I did not rush out to consult with any human being. -Galatians 1:13-16

No matter what you've done if you honestly know and admit that you are a sinner who needs deliverance, believe that Jesus is God, believe that he came to die in place of you to save you from your sins, believe he was buried in a tomb and was resurrected three days later, and approach the Lord Jesus with true remorse and sincere repentance then surrender your life to him you will have salvation.

Later on, after John was arrested, Jesus went into Galilee, where he preached God's Good News.

"The time promised by God has come at last!" he announced. "The Kingdom of God is near! Repent of your sins and believe

the Good News!" -Mark 1:14-15

But now God has shown us a way to be made right with him without keeping the requirements of the law, as was promised in the writings of Moses and the prophets long ago.

We are made right with God by placing our faith in Jesus Christ.

And this is true for everyone who believes, no matter who we are.

For everyone has sinned; we all fall short of God's glorious standard.

Yet God, in his grace, freely makes us right in his sight.

He did this through Christ Jesus when he freed us from the penalty for our sins.

For God presented Jesus as the sacrifice for sin. People are made right with God when they believe that Jesus sacrificed his life, shedding his blood.

This sacrifice shows that God was being fair when he held back and did not punish those who sinned in times past, for he was looking ahead and including them in what he would do in this present time.

God did this to demonstrate his righteousness, for he himself is fair and just, and he makes sinners right in his sight when they believe in Jesus.

Can we boast, then, that we have done anything to be accepted by God? No, because our acquittal is not based on obeying the law.

It is based on faith. So we are made right with God through faith and not by obeying the law.

After all, is God the God of the Jews only? Isn't he also the God of the Gentiles?

Of course he is. There is only one God, and he makes people right with himself only by faith, whether they are Jews or Gentiles.

Well then, if we emphasize faith, does this mean that we can forget about the law? Of course not! In fact, only when we have faith do we truly fulfill the law. -Romans 3:21-31

All praise to God, the Father of our Lord Jesus Christ, who has blessed us with every spiritual blessing in the heavenly realms because we are united with Christ.

Even before he made the world, God loved us and chose us in Christ to be holy and without fault in his eyes. God decided in advance to adopt us into his own family by bringing us to himself through Jesus Christ.

This is what he wanted to do, and it gave him great pleasure.

So we praise God for the glorious grace he has poured out on us who belong to his dear Son.

He is so rich in kindness and grace that he purchased our freedom with the blood of his Son and forgave our sins. He has showered his kindness on us, along with all wisdom and understanding. -Ephesians 1:3-8

* * *

A God Of Mercy And Compassion

Are you in a dark or difficult place right now?

Do you question whether God really loves you and find it hard to believe that he actually does?

Have you ever said to yourself or thought, "If God cared about me, he wouldn't have allowed me to come into this world and be put through all kinds of unsavory experiences?

If so, you are not alone. Many people feel this way and have felt this way.

Take heart, there is indeed a God up there in the heavens who is also all around us as well as inside of us- those of us who are his children (*who he gave the right to become sons and daughters -john 1:12*)- who loves us dearly.

Psalms 103:8-19 says, The LORD is compassionate and

merciful, slow to get angry and filled with unfailing love.

He will not constantly accuse us, nor remain angry forever. He does not punish us for all our sins; he does not deal harshly with us, as we deserve. For his unfailing love toward those who fear him is as great as the height of the heavens above the earth. He has removed our sins as far from us as the east is from the west.

The LORD is like a father to his children, tender and compassionate to those who fear him. For he knows how weak we are; he remembers we are only dust. Our days on earth are like grass; like wildflowers, we bloom and die.

The wind blows, and we are gone— as though we had never been here. But the love of the LORD remains forever with those who fear him. His salvation extends to the children's children of those who are faithful to his covenant, of those who obey his commandments! The LORD has made the heavens his throne; from there he rules over everything.

* * *

God Knows All, So Come To Know Him

O LORD, you have examined my heart and know everything about me. You know when I sit down or stand up.

You know my thoughts even when I'm far away. You see me when I travel and when I rest at home.

You know everything I do. You know what I am going to say even before I say it, LORD.

You go before me and follow me. You place your hand of blessing on my head.

Such knowledge is too wonderful for me, too great for me to understand! I can never escape from your Spirit! I can never get away from your presence! -Psalms 139:1-7

What is done behind closed doors and in front of mirrors can be kept hidden unseen from others, and put far behind as to never have existed.

The walls of a room will never talk, the doors of a room will never open up to reveal anything that ever took place, and the mirrors within a room will never again reflect a scene displayed from the past.

One can even lie to them self, denying what no one else could prove unless there was substantial evidence or a credible witness.

The truth would be portrayed as a lie for as long as one continued to not admit, or forget.

Going back inside the rooms through the doors to look back into the mirrors sometimes can force or incite one to face a reality they may not prefer to accept.

The fact that even though actions and things will sometimes be or remain unknown to anyone else- it is still definitely known.

God knows.

No matter how hard one tries, how hard one runs, how hard one pretends they can never escape the one who is aware of all things.

No one can masquerade or play a charade on God.

Stop running, trying, and/or pretending and confess to the Lord what he already knows so that he may give you a peace, comfort and joy that the world does not give, understand, and is unable to take away.

Why carry a burden when you do not have to.

Our good Lord is ever so merciful and full of grace. He is just waiting for anyone to come to him as he is ready to forgive, forget, and fulfill with a life of restoration and purpose to all those who surrender to his everlasting love and divine perfection.

But if we confess our sins to him, he is faithful and just to forgive us our sins and to cleanse us from all wickedness. -1 John 1:9

Nine

Endurance

I do not take anything for granted. I am always thankful and grateful within the ways that I am blessed.

All throughout my life I have noticed how God has taken very good cared of me. He has been constant and extremely consistent.

I look at some people who are unfortunate in their situations, life is uncertain and we never know what predicament may come upon us.

It is rational to wonder and to think ahead, especially with so many unpredictable things that often take place.

However, we are not to worry, and we are not to compare ourselves to others using their circumstance as a maybe of what can happen to us- even though things do sometimes happen.

Yet, many things that seem tragic do not necessarily promote a negative outcome.

When a door closes a window opens and sometimes it is just time to move on to a higher path upon our journey.

The Lord does bring good out of the bad events that occur within our lives.

Things come along to refine us, enhance our growth, and to makes us even stronger to accomplish what we are put here to do on earth until we return to our final eternal home.

We are to always put our hope and faith in God.

My inner-voice of spirit speaks to me whenever in doubt, or within concern about something. It lets me know that everything is going to be okay.

From experience I have no choice but to accept this truth and to keep moving forward. There is no other option.

The Lord fulfills on his promises to never leave, abandon, or fail to provide.

I have a strong relationship with God, one with a long history of incredible things received beyond expectation.

With the Lord there within me, beside me, and everywhere

around me I am safe and secure knowing that my future and more is already being worked out for my preparation and advancement into a greater intention.

I have a happiness when there should be sadness. I have peace and relaxation when there should be worry or anxiety.

I have entertainment and enjoyment when I should have boredom and disgust.

Why? Because I am supposed to as a human creature who is in this world but definitely not of it!

I learned years ago from my encounters that a strong faith sees the invisible, believes the impossible, and receives the incredible.

Life can be hard and discouraging at times and within moments, nevertheless we have the comforter who holds all things together then motivates us into action so that we can keep running this race with endurance.

* * *

A Change Of Heart

I have heard stories of how Jesus transformed prostitutes, drug addicts, murderers, and so on.

I have never been any of those things, but for the Lord to

actually impact the lives of specific individuals who once lived within the grips of that type of lifestyle is truly inspiring and phenomenal.

I can testify to how God transformed my heart from hatred toward him to amicable.

I believe aside for his great purpose for me the Lord also wants to use me as an example and inspiration to others.

If he could rededicate a believer of him since childhood who turned away from him in animosity during adulthood that is a story worth telling within itself- no matter how minor it may seem.

Returning back to the arms of God, surrendering completely to his plan, and having a hunger for reading the word and connecting deeper to his spirit is hardly anything insignificant to the Lord.

The event is a cause for celebration in the heavens. There is nothing more important on earth than having an intimate partnership with God.

* * *

Standing Strong In Christ

For the LORD watches over the path of the godly, but the path

of the wicked leads to destruction. -Psalms 1:6

When we trust in God and follow his lead, we appear foolish to others sometimes.

There are occasionally going to be those cruel people who may criticize or attack you out of ignorance, a sick mentality, or just from their own feelings of insecurity and inadequacy.

Do not allow yourself to be injured or discouraged by the actions they direct toward you.

Their words and behavior are irrelevant, purely a reflection of themselves and the road they are traveling down.

There is no need to pay attention to, or to give any energy to anything other than the estimation that God has of you. **-You saw me before I was born. Every day of my life was recorded in your book. Every moment was laid out before a single day had passed. How precious are your thoughts about me, O God? They cannot be numbered! -Psalms 139:16-17**

If God puts it in your heart to do something, do not hesitate to do it and if the Lord wants you to be a witness for him do not be afraid to declare your testimony in front of others.

I am not saying to go around making a boisterous show among others I am urging you to never feel uncomfortable walking according to your faith.

When you are among others, do you let them know that you

love and follow your creator if the opportunity presents itself?

Do you acknowledge your desire to not do what goes against your beliefs when questioned or faced in a situation?

Do you acknowledge your love for Christian music over secular music?

Do you read your biblical content openly in front of them?

Would you pray in front of them without embarrassment if the moment called for it?

If anyone is ashamed of me and my message in these adulterous and sinful days, the Son of Man will be ashamed of that person when he returns in the glory of his Father with the holy angels."
-Mark 8:38

* * *

Standing Out From The Crowd

Oh, the joys of those who do not follow the advice of the wicked, or stand around with sinners, or join in with mockers. But they delight in the law of the Lord , meditating on it day and night.
Psalms 1:1-2

Do you get criticized or downgraded for who you are and what you believe in?

Do certain others harass you and try to intimidate you because you don't follow their crowd or way of life?

If the answer to these questions is a yes then be proud and stand your ground!

Do not give in and do not give up on yourself.

Do not look for the acceptance or approval of others who do not show you any courtesy or respect.

You are not defined by any of their belittling words or irrelevant opinions.

If you find yourself to be the outcast within this situation- cut off from the rest or more popular- prefer to stay that way!

Keep doing what you do and just be you.

There will come people your way who will share your interests and connect with you on a particular level if you choose.

In the meantime, savor your alone time building a relationship with the true leader who stood out from the crowd of narrow-minded people to never fit in.

Do not go with the narrow points of view yet stay on the straight and narrow path and view.

My Creative Biblical Prayer through verse: *Thank you father in heaven for planting me like trees along your riverbank, and allowing* *me to bear fruit each season.*

My leaves never wither and they prosper in all they do.

In your precious son, Jesus name Amen.

Ten

Fear/Worry

❧

Rest In The Lord

The LORD is a shelter for the oppressed, a refuge in times of trouble. Those who know your name trust in you, for you, O LORD, do not abandon those who search for you. Psalms 9:9-10

Yes, we live in an unpredictable world. A problem or tragedy can hit at any time.

It is tiring and unhealthy to constantly panic about events that are entirely out of our control.

Anxiety will drive one to become restless and stress will cause one to suffer ill health.

Just give it to God and let him handle whatever it is that is going on in your life whether good or bad.

Isn't it so much better to sit back, relax, and totally allow the Lord to steer your ship?

We sail with comfort to enjoy a much better ride than if we ourselves were the ones in charge to operate.

Not only is God our ultimate guide but he is the one source that is able to provide definite stability and confidence within any uncertain situation.

And this same God who takes care of me will supply all your needs from his glorious riches, which have been given to us in Christ Jesus. -Philippians 4:19

* * *

A Feeling Of Fear

But when I am afraid, I will put my trust in you. -Psalms 56:3

A little while back, I was feeling a wave of fear and I told a woman who use to be a neighbor of mine.

In response, she told me to pray and ask about it. Then, wait for an answer.

So, I did. I prayed to the Lord that night, expressing my concern and any possible reason in particular for why I was experiencing this stream of fear.

When I awoke the next morning, I had initially forgot about the prayer and reply I had requested.

Once I remembered, an answer had actually come into my mind.

A voice spoke to me in my thoughts and said, "Have a little bit more faith in God".

There it was. Plain and simple for my specific situation.

All of us are different, all going through our various seasons of life.

While we experience these shifts in motion and change, we may also encounter a touch of fear or uncertainty.

It is understandable, especially not knowing where our season may be weathering to, but the most important thing for us to know is that God is the one controlling the environment.

He orders the summer, the fall, the winter, and the spring.

He'll keep us warm when it's cold.

And he'll keep us comfortable when things get too hot for us to handle.

God is there, even when he seems far away.

He just wants us to have the faith to trust him when we can't see past the fog.

Let God be the eyes we view our circumstances with as he already knows what's upon and ahead, he will lead us through.

For we live by believing and not by seeing. -2 Corinthians 5:7

* * *

Satan's Idling

Upon waking up one morning, a voice in my thoughts spoke to me and said, "Don't pay any attention to God.

Immediately, I knew it was the voice of the enemy. I did not listen to the nonsense of those words at all.

The devil and his demons will always endeavor to put lies and doubts into our minds suddenly to confuse or misdirect us, no matter how ludicrous or trivial the attempt may seem.

Satan and his army have zero power over us because Jesus conquered long ago, however, they will still mess with us from time to time.

Stay alert! Watch out for your great enemy, the devil.

He prowls around like a roaring lion, looking for someone to devour. Stand firm against him, and be strong in your faith.

Remember that your family of believers all over the world is going through the same kind of suffering you are. -1 Peter 5:8-9

Eleven

Sorrow/Mourning

The LORD is close to the brokenhearted; he rescues those whose spirits are crushed. -Psalms 34:18

I know it hurts so much when you lose someone you cared for to death.

The more you loved that person the more pain you feel.

It is so beautiful and dreadful at the same time.

The beauty lies within the affection, the dread lies within the separation.

Though nothing can ease the injury that reflects from the

broken heart may there be the comfort in knowing for the believer and those who believed that their beloved is now within a better place.

Yes, we grieve and are heavily bereaved because we miss them so dearly.

But it was in God's will and maybe he took them home to release them from any further suffering.

Nevertheless, our departed are in the best hands of our Lord and savior/heavenly father.

Also, let there be comfort in knowing that one day we will be reunited with the ones we loved- and there will be no more sadness, no more crying, no more pain and no more death.

Only love, peace, and happiness forever more.

All praise to God, the Father of our Lord Jesus Christ. It is by his great mercy that we have been born again, because God raised Jesus Christ from the dead.

Now we live with great expectation, and we have a priceless inheritance—an inheritance that is kept in heaven for you, pure and undefiled, beyond the reach of change and decay.

And through your faith, God is protecting you by his power until you receive this salvation, which is ready to be revealed on the last day for all to see.

So be truly glad. There is wonderful joy ahead, even though you must endure many trials for a little while.

These trials will show that your faith is genuine. It is being tested as fire tests and purifies gold—though your faith is far more precious than mere gold.

So when your faith remains strong through many trials, it will bring you much praise and glory and honor on the day when Jesus Christ is revealed to the whole world.

You love him even though you have never seen him. Though you do not see him now, you trust him; and you rejoice with a glorious, inexpressible joy. The reward for trusting him will be the salvation of your souls. 1 Peter 1:3-9

Twelve

Anointed/Healing

Ministering Angels

Therefore, angels are only servants—spirits sent to care for people who will inherit salvation. -Hebrews 1:14

One night before bed, years ago, I lit a candle on the floor beside my bed.

I had never lit a candle on the floor beside my bed before.

Normally, if I lit one, I would put the glass encased candle upon the dresser or bureau, a safer place.

I don't know what I was thinking at the time. And this wasn't a glass encased candle. It was a small white votive candle.

Anyhow, during the night I was sleeping very sound and comfortably when a divine touch awakened me, raised up my head and turned me around to see my blanket and sheet on fire just in time.

The grasp that was held onto me was gentle yet alerting, I'll never forget the incident.

For the angel of the LORD is a guard; he surrounds and defends all who fear him. -Psalms 34:7

God's mighty and powerful hand has been on me for all of my life and it is a shame how I couldn't see how much he loved me back then.

Going through things and the trials in life can alter our view of God especially when trauma is involved.

Satan plays his part too by lying to us, trying to manipulate us to think and believe God is against us.

Nevertheless, God has supernaturally intervened on my behalf a number of times in my life and it has built a strong faith and shaped me.

Daniel answered, "Long live the king! My God sent his angel to shut the lions' mouths so that they would not hurt me, for I have been found innocent in his sight. And I have not wronged you, Your Majesty." -Daniel 6:21-22

* * *

God's Healing Touch

O LORD, if you heal me, I will be truly healed; if you save me, I will be truly saved. My praises are for you alone! Jeremiah 17:14

In 1984, my grandmother had a stroke. She remained in coma for three months and some presumed that she would eventually die.

A few associates of my mother's told her to take me up to the hospital to see my grandmother, that maybe my presence could wake her up somehow, I guess.

One day my mother did take me to the hospital to visit my grandmother and I touched her hand and held it, and my grandmother awakened after three months of being in a comatose state.

Now I know that I myself didn't have any power to actually bring my grandmother back to consciousness, but I know that God did because he wasn't ready for my grandmother to have left the earth yet.

But I believe he may have intervened through my touch as he divinely works through who he chooses.

I was a child back then so maybe God had his reasons I don't know and cannot say for sure why the incident transpired the way it did. I thought it was a beautiful moment, though.

It may have been a little faith on my part too for the Lord to wake my grandma up, it was so long ago I do not remember if I prayed for her or not but I do think I remember anticipating and believing she could wake up because others were encouraging my visit to her.

My grandmother recovered quite well and made very good improvements a while afterwards when she returned home.

I recall some women came to my grandmother to pray over her and to aid her in accepting Jesus as her Lord and savior.

She wasn't one hundred percent incapacitated as one side of her body was permanently paralyzed.

However, she was in her right mind, she was able to cook for herself, dress herself, wheel herself around the house, and she was able to verbally communicate with us (her family and others).

She just had a slight memory impairment as she knew what she wanted to say yet couldn't get out some of her words but we articulated what she wanted to convey.

My grandmother lived another twenty years after the onset of her stroke, she probably would have lived longer if she hadn't later on developed lung cancer from continuing to smoke.

Everyone tried to touch him, because healing power went out from him, and he healed everyone. -Luke 6:19

Thirteen

People/The World

Underestimated By People? Never By God!

For we are God's masterpiece. He has created us anew in Christ Jesus, so we can do the good things he planned for us long ago. Ephesians 2:10

Isn't it something how certain people will judge you by social status, or measure your worth or success by what type of job or material possessions you may have or own?

A lot of individuals tend to go by what they see on the outside of a person's life and what they know by what has been revealed about them.

But what about the realities of that person which have not been showed to those individuals and circumstances not yet unveiled to them?

Does not knowing about another person's attributes or capabilities make them any less capable or valuable? Absolutely not!

There are people walking around in high positions and gaining notoriety for things they didn't actually earn or deserve.

If a person has not reached a particular level of achievement within life it does not mean or signify that they aren't sufficient or talented enough in the specific area whatever that may be.

True success is not based on the opinions and desires of the world.

It does not matter what shifting individuals think or believe about us. It only matters what God knows about us.

The Lord created each and every one of us with a unique purpose to carry out. He gave us all that was required within our gifts, talents and abilities to perform our mission.

It is not up to anyone but God to determine what success means for the life we were given.

By his divine power, God has given us everything we need for living a godly life.

We have received all of this by coming to know him, the one who called us to himself by means of his marvelous glory and excellence.

And because of his glory and excellence, he has given us great and precious promises.

These are the promises that enable you to share his divine nature and escape the world's corruption caused by human desires. -2 Peter 1:3-4

* * *

True Christian Behavior

But God's truth stands firm like a foundation stone with this inscription: "The LORD knows those who are his," and "All who belong to the LORD must turn away from evil." 2 Timothy 2:19

But when people keep on sinning, it shows that they belong to the devil, who has been sinning since the beginning.

But the Son of God came to destroy the works of the devil. Those who have been born into God's family do not make a practice of sinning, because God's life is in them.

So they can't keep on sinning, because they are children of God. So now we can tell who are children of God and who are

children of the devil. Anyone who does not live righteously and does not love other believers does not belong to God. 1 John 3:8-10

The house of the wicked will be destroyed, but the tent of the godly will flourish. There is a path before each person that seems right, but it ends in death. Proverbs 14:11-12

When we become saved (a born again Christian) God's holy spirit comes to literally dwell within us. ***Don't you realize that your body is the temple of the Holy Spirit, who lives in you and was given to you by God? You do not belong to yourself - 1 Corinthians 6:19***

The spirit is our helper and comforter.

Not only does God endow us with supernatural abilities (spiritual gifts) he divinely enables us to become holy by gradually perfecting/changing us in Jesus Christ's image.

We will never be flawless within our fleshly bodies in this fallen world and we will at times sin, however, our sin will be less and it won't be constant or intentional.

During those periods we may suddenly or accidentally slip up, we acknowledge our error to God and receive his forgiveness. Always requesting in him that he aid us to improve.

No one sincere takes the Lord's grace and mercy for granted, knowing that he blessed us within this way should encourage us to look forward with appreciation and motivation to cooperate.

The true Christian does not practice sin as a way of life. The way of life puts sin out of practice.

Anyone who claims to be living in the spirit yet does worldly things routinely is not a legitimate follower who surrendered to Christ.

When embraced by the holy spirit, everything starts to change- desires, thoughts, personality and foundation.

One's entire manner of being has become refashioned. God's essence brings a purity to the presence.

I knew a man years ago when I was a young child, I think I was around ten or eleven (around that time I had accepted Jesus).

He was an associate of my family.

He used to treat me funny until one day he came to my home and witnessed me reading my bible.

I don't know what his problem was, I was just a kid.

Anyway, this married man called himself a person of God and of the church, but would come over to my house asking if he could use our VCR (this was back in the 1980's) to watch porn tapes he had brought over.

He also pinched one of my mother's friends on her derriere at the staircase.

Now my point is also that he acted negative toward me for a while and I hadn't done anything to him but it was alright for him to fulfill his lustful desires apart from his wife.

Typical judgmental so called/false Christian behavior.

This is why so many professing Christians/followers of Christ leave a bad taste in other people's mouths and bad impressions of what true Christians are and represent.

It used to be said that the worse kinds of people are the ones in the church.

Whether some deserved that reputation or not depending on opinion the main focus of everything is to get it together with God because only he can make things right for everyone.

My dear children, I am writing this to you so that you will not sin.

But if anyone does sin, we have an advocate who pleads our case before the Father.

He is Jesus Christ, the one who is truly righteous. He himself is the sacrifice that atones for our sins—and not only our sins but the sins of all the world.

And we can be sure that we know him if we obey his commandments. If someone claims, "I know God," but doesn't obey God's commandments, that person is a liar and is not living in the truth.

But those who obey God's word truly show how completely they love him. That is how we know we are living in him. Those who say they live in God should live their lives as Jesus did. -1 John 2:1-6

Dear friends, you always followed my instructions when I was with you. And now that I am away, it is even more important.

Work hard to show the results of your salvation, obeying God with deep reverence and fear. For God is working in you, giving you the desire and the power to do what pleases him. Philippians 2:12-13

For God wanted them to know that the riches and glory of Christ are for you Gentiles, too.

And this is the secret: Christ lives in you. This gives you assurance of sharing his glory.

So we tell others about Christ, warning everyone and teaching everyone with all the wisdom God has given us. We want to present them to God, perfect in their relationship to Christ.

That's why I work and struggle so hard, depending on Christ's mighty power that works within me. -Colossians 1:27-29

Fourteen

Identity

True Identity And Self-Worth

For the LORD God is our sun and our shield. He gives us grace and glory. The LORD will withhold no good thing from those who do what is right. Psalms 84:11

I was loved immensely by my mother and I had an overwhelming sense of divine providence around me that contributed to the beneficial state of my well being.

I never cared if others liked, loved, or respected me because how others treated or felt about me whether good or bad had no actual relevance to my true value and worth.

My self-esteem did not come from how anyone defined me, it never did, and it never will!

I had a favor on my life that I noticed and that was noticed by certain others. This is where my value and worth originated.

Within the power of the highest who adores, nurtures, and provides me with every essential need for growth and eternal sustainability.

God loved and cared for me during times when I wasn't even sure or aware of his absolute concern for me.

Yes, I went through a period of doubt as I believed the Lord was against me and out to get me through the misinterpretation that I had of him from going through hardships at a very early age.

While I thought God was cruel and barbaric, and depended upon and gave praise and honor to other spiritual "notions" within the "universe" who seem to have kept me safe, assured, and supported it was indeed the Lord all along there by my side who shined his wonderful light where I could not see.

What a great, faithful, loving and merciful father we have dwelling up within the heavens.

He truly is exceptional.

And, I am exceptionally secure and confident within myself through his blessings. I am most humbled and grateful by this supernatural experience.

Thank you, my Lord. I love you Jesus!

"What is the price of five sparrows—two copper coins?

Yet God does not forget a single one of them. And the very hairs on your head are all numbered.

So don't be afraid; you are more valuable to God than a whole flock of sparrows. -Luke 12:6-7

* * *

The View Of Different Sins

All wicked actions are sin, but not every sin leads to death.

We know that God's children do not make a practice of sinning, for God's Son holds them securely, and the evil one cannot touch them.

We know that we are children of God and that the world around us is under the control of the evil one. -1 John 5:17-19

Many of us have a view of sin that does not align up with God's view of sin.

We separate sin to degree when all sin is forbidden, intolerable and detestable to the Lord.

Most of us would not consider telling what we may define as a little white lie within the same category as to kill or murder someone.

It is fair to suggest that a little white lie is far less terrible than to commit a murder.

Yet, little lies can turn into big lies and, lies in general can get people killed depending on what is said and what is believed.

Nevertheless, telling someone you like their cooked meal or outfit when you really do not, does not at all equal up to the severity of taking another person's life or raping someone, and so on.

It is better not to comment at all in a situation if possible or to just be honest within a polite way when you disagree with something or are not interested.

This form of action would keep God happy!

Of course, we as imperfect humans are going to sometimes sin.

All sin leads to hell.

We must constantly pray, repent, and ask God for his forgiveness, assistance and intervention.

If it was not for Jesus Christ everyone would be in severe trouble!

* * *

The Love Of God

But you, O Lord, are a God of compassion and mercy, slow to get angry and filled with unfailing love and faithfulness. -Psalms 86:15

For the LORD your God is living among you. He is a mighty savior. He will take delight in you with gladness. With his love, he will calm all your fears. He will rejoice over you with joyful songs." -Zephaniah 3:17

God's love is beyond our comprehension.

He loves us more than anyone else could ever imagine, and he loves our loved ones more than we would ever be capable.
This kind of love is outstanding and unsurpassed.
A lot of us may believe that God doesn't love or care about us, and that he is distant from us through certain seasons of life.
However, we are instructed to walk by faith. We are to depend on the word of God and not on our feelings when it comes to the character and nature of our Lord.
Always read the scriptures in the bible whenever in doubt or in need for encouragement. And, always resort to the word of God for daily living and guidance.
Talk to God in prayer about anything, constantly thanking him for everything that he has done and that he continues to do for you.

See how very much our Father loves us, for he calls us his children, and that is what we are! But the people who belong to this world don't recognize that we are God's children because they don't know him. - *1 John 3:1*

But God showed his great love for us by sending Christ to die for us while we were still sinners. -*Romans 5:8*

But God is so rich in mercy, and he loved us so much, that even though we were dead because of our sins, he gave us life when he raised Christ from the dead. (It is only by God's grace that you have been saved!) -*Ephesians 2:4-5*

"For this is how God loved the world: He gave his one and only Son, so that everyone who believes in him will not perish but have eternal life. -*John 3:16*

God showed how much he loved us by sending his one and only Son into the world so that we might have eternal life through him.

This is real love—not that we loved God, but that he loved us and sent his Son as a sacrifice to take away our sins. Dear friends, since God loved us that much, we surely ought to love each other. -*1 John 4:9-11*

We know how much God loves us, and we have put our trust in his love. God is love, and all who live in love live in God, and God lives in them. *1 John 4:16*

Fifteen

Time For God Before It Is Too Late

There is no such thing as not having the time to talk to God or not being able to fit God into one's schedule.

We are able to communicate with God at any second, minute, or hour of the day at any moment, any place, and during any circumstance.

There is no situation where or when God cannot be reached or spoken to.

We can contact God upon waking up, taking a shower, brushing our teeth, eating, heading out the door, driving, riding public transportation, working, or even in the middle of a conversation with another person.

It only takes a thought directed to the creator in which he

automatically hears and knows beforehand.

We do not even have to open up our mouths to talk to God. He is all around us and for those of us who are saved his Holy Spirit he lives inside of us.

There is absolutely no excuse to not communicate with God when it comes to engaging in a dedicated relationship with him.

There are no fancy words to use just whatever is on our mind.

God is our father/parent, we go to him as his children for any and everything. There is nothing too big and nothing too small.

There is a difference between having the spare quality time to read or study the bible and actually speaking our words to God.

Yes, we may have to make time for reading but there is always time to talk.

* * *

Once Again In A Year

There Is Purpose To Our Life

*For we are God's masterpiece. He has created us anew in Christ Jesus, so we can do the good things he planned for us long ago. -**Ephesians 2:10***

There is nothing special about a new year within itself. It is just a regular ongoing natural spectrum of time, an inevitable unstoppable occurrence among us as we live day by day.

The only thing truly special about a new year is the fact that we are still here into the onset of the next 12 months to fulfill our purpose on the planet.

Every day that we have life is a new day to start fresh. Fresh in whatever brings us closer into our relationship with God and the newness of refreshing our spirits to the glorification of being made holy.

* * *

The Why Question?

I heard a long time ago from someone that we as people are not supposed to ask "why?"

I disagree.

Why not ask "why" to a lot of the things and situations that are going on and that are taking place within life.

We all know the story of the devil being kicked out of heaven, and about Adam and Eve disobeying God and getting kicked out of the garden.

Still, what about all of the people who did not ask to be born to come into this world the way that things turned out.

It is not everyone else's fault what happened beforehand.

I have asked and wondered why too.

Why as to certain things regardless of how much scripture I have read, how many incredible experiences I have had with God, or how deep my spiritual gifts ran.

There are questions we need answers to, unexplainable events and occurrences that are inexcusable to our understanding.

Like why does God allow innocent babies to get raped, beaten, and murdered when he can instantly wipe out the existence of any human being or creature on the planet and beyond?

How is preventing a baby from getting hurt interfering with someone else's free will?

And, if it does interfere what is the big deal when it is to save a child or any innocent individual from being harmed?

This is just one of many examples of happenings to be pondered and discussed.

I am not trying to knock God it is just one of those why questions that we sometimes ask.

Some may say who are we to question God, but the Lord gave

us minds to think with, thoughts to deliberate, and mouths to speak and to make inquiries with.

We are not guaranteed every answer to all of our questions here on this earth, yet the Lord welcomes us to seek him with all of our hearts and to not be afraid to ask for wisdom.

Must I forever see these evil deeds?

Why must I watch all this misery? Wherever I look, I see destruction and violence.

I am surrounded by people who love to argue and fight. The law has become paralyzed, and there is no justice in the courts.

The wicked far outnumber the righteous, so that justice has become perverted. -Habakkuk 1:3-4

Now we see things imperfectly, like puzzling reflections in a mirror, but then we will see everything with perfect clarity.

All that I know now is partial and incomplete, but then I will know everything completely, just as God now knows me completely. -1 Corinthians 13:12

If you need wisdom, ask our generous God, and he will give it to you. He will not rebuke you for asking.

But when you ask him, be sure that your faith is in God alone. Do not waver, for a person with divided loyalty is as unsettled as a wave of the sea that is blown and tossed by the wind. -James

1:5-6

* * *

If He Says It Then It Will Be Done

"Everything will be alright".

Those words are easier said and heard than registered, especially when we are going through a discouraging, difficult, or dark time or season.

Nevertheless, if God says our situation will turn out fine (or for the best) and that we will be okay then it absolutely shall be as he said.

It has been this way for me constantly within my life so I speak from experience, and to give inspiration and assurance that our Lord is consistent.

The Lord replied, "I will personally go with you, Moses, and I will give you rest—everything will be fine for you." -Exodus 33:14